fall

Also by Amy Newman

Order, or Disorder (1995)
Camera Lyrica (1999)

fall

Amy Newman

Wesleyan University Press

Middletown, Connecticut

Published by Wesleyan University Press, Middletown, CT 06459
© 2004 by Amy Newman

ISBN 0-8195-6708-6 cloth
Printed in the United States of America

Grateful acknowledgments to the editors of the following journals in which
these poems first appeared: *American Letters & Commentary, Bellingham
Review, Colorado Review, The Georgia Review, Image, Itinera, Hotel Amerika,
The Journal, The Laurel Review, The Missouri Review, Seneca Review,*
and *West Branch*.

The dictionary definitions for "fall" and "prayer" are from *The American Heritage Dictionary*. Copyright © 1981 by Houghton Mifflin Company. Reproduced
by permission from *The American Heritage Dictionary, New College Edition*.

Excerpt from "The First Elegy" from *The Duino Elegies* by Rainer Maria Rilke,
translated by Edward Snow. Translation copyright © 2000 by Edward Snow.
Reprinted by permission of North Point Press, a division of Farrar, Straus and
Giroux, LLC.

I am grateful to the Illinois Arts Council, Northern Illinois University, and The
MacDowell Colony for material support and time to complete the manuscript.
Gratitude also to Mona Marshall and Jill Nelson, who supported the spirit
throughout the third section. This book would not exist without Joe Bonomo,
to whom it is devoted.

Design and composition by Julie Allred, BW&A Books, Inc., Durham, N.C.

Cataloging-in-Publication Data appear
on the last printed page of the book

5 4 3 2 1

for Tom Andrews
for Dad

fall (fôl) v. **fell** (fĕl), **fallen** (fôʹlən), **falling, falls.** —*intr.* intransitive. To move under the influence of gravity; especially, to drop without restraint. To come to rest; strike bottom; land: *The world first fell from the firmament.* To drop oneself from an erect to a less erect position: *He stumbled and fell.* To hang down: *Eve's hair fell in ringlets.* To be conquered or seized. To yield to temptation; To err or sin. To lose one's chastity. Used especially of a woman. Appendix[a]. Appendix[b]. To assume an expression of disappointment: *His Face fell.* To undergo a reduction in amount, degree, or value; To diminish. To divide naturally. Used with *into*: *The specimens fell into three categories.* Appendix[c]. —*tr.* transitive. —**fall back.** To give ground; recede; retreat. —**fall for.** *Informal.* **1.** To become infatuated with; fall suddenly in love with. **2.** To be tricked or deceived by; be taken in by. —**fall among.** To come by chance into the company of. —**fall behind.** To be in arrears. —**fall on** (or **upon**). To attack suddenly; ambush. —**fall away. 1.** To decline; languish; weaken. **2.** To withdraw support; part company. —**fall under.** To succumb to; come under an influence or power. —**fall foul.** To become entangled. —**fall flat.** *Informal.* To fail completely to achieve the intended effect. —**fall back on** (or **upon**). **1.** To retreat to. **2.** To resort to. —**fall in with.** To come to an agreement. —**fall to. 1.** To begin (a physical activity) energetically. **2.** To shut or move into place by itself. —*n.* noun. That which has fallen. Usually capital **F.** *Theology.* Adam's sin of disobeying God by eating the forbidden fruit in the Garden of Eden, and the consequent loss of innocence and grace of all his descendants. A sudden drop from a relatively erect to a less erect position: *He fell to his knees.* An ornamental cascade of lace or trimming attached to the dress, usually at the collar. The amount of what has fallen. The end of a cable, rope, or chain that is pulled by the power source in hoisting. The act or instance of falling; a dropping down; free descent. The birth of an animal, especially, the birth of a lamb. Appendix[d]. Appendix[e]. A downward movement or a slope. Often capital **F.** Autumn.

how little at home we are in the interpreted world
Rainer Maria Rilke

Contents

fall

To move under the influence of gravity;
especially, to drop without restraint.

The eyes close and the gilded flesh
leaves messages in its spiraling, leaves
us astounded at the festive lethargy, at the body's
reckless, pliant, beautiful lessening,

a shedding of the eye level of things—
tinny cascade of objects, and the dailiness—
then the weight of all that blood and flesh, the fully human
and bright limbs thinking their way

to the pavement, to the grass, to the water
at the root of the world, all that
thinking, *I am falling,* and the requisite dull hit
and the end of the defining. A body falls like a story:

beginning, middle, end. I am watching as she falls,
an equation: the earth's rotation cleaved
as if by insects by this tiniest shift of breath,
the angle of the downward motion

factored in wing beat against the world's rushing curve.
A beautiful woman falls against the scrim, the tiny distance,
shoulders almost fold as a neat clean blouse,
rib cage dropped in gentle descent, musical,

the decrescendo, her diminution, this whisper added
to the world's weight. Natural, artful,
the body falls. First height, then loss, all the way down:
the earth the only friend to catch you, the hard truth, the helpful ending.

intransitive

To come to rest; strike bottom; land:
The world first fell from the firmament.

In the beginning. Out of the most original begins the world,
its wish of industry, the main idea,
this first weather, a breeze across God's face,
new craft swifting, moored, in the unharbored sky.

While we were in effort dreamed—a wordless dream of evers,
the still un-world buzzing in a magnet's pull,
humming our eyes swift under their translucence, images
in slow motion—while we were dreamed, the world's solid shape

pulled its mathematical issue from the density of sky,
the filaments of matter in their depth, dirt, color.
And out of this we must have arrived, without luggage.
What would be our eventual.
A sweet primary shift to the ordered world.

When I lean in, I feel a fibrous answer,
the burden of the heart hanging in its chest, a little fruit,
and it hurts with its tiny weight, the logarithm
of the pre-made world—the pre-world
firmament, soft, inviting, into which—

by invitation, or uninvited—we
spread ourselves among the Eden. Raised
to its first power. Into that temperate, unfocused place,
entwined as promise beneath the trees, we arrived,
the fallible human material.

> To drop oneself from an erect to a less erect position:
> *He stumbled and fell.*

Adam tussled with the animals, he dreamt beneath
the cherry woods, believed the grasses *soft*
(though there was no word for it)
and their hides textured: *bark* (though this was abstract)
and the roots, over which,
as he stumbled and fell, *extension* —

as landscape descended
blue and swift, and he would think
I am startled by beauty, by this mere
trick of permanence, the moving of things
in their upward heft, their running away
as I tumble downward, the serious, rich blur of the coherent world:

(bird)
            / first dove second dove third rush of dove

(flight)
            / white gray steel blue violet of tailfeather

(image)
            / dress of vein and feather, swift as a tongue

Released from the mouth, language
simplifies in air, polishing the genuine.
Adam imagines:
rest, avian, warmth, hollow, fill, kiss, dream, woman.

To hang down:
Eve's hair fell in ringlets.

Now they were quiet, so he leans in and says to her—
this is not the first joke, he leans in and before he can speak—
the shape of her face as it profiles, like a lost child
the ear a burden to him, it hurts to see the curve
and its restless volute, her semicircular canals
like a polished bed in some fragrant idea of lovemaking—
he could name her, starting at her petaled feet,
her toes, the little carapace
of nail, hard to his hard,
all that dream of leg and scent, he knows her—
what if he takes her to him? To name:
all the parts of her. Doesn't she think to smile? But her face
is dynamic as sound, the reach of it like
a missed letter. He can glance her pelvis into several
names, her inheritance of muscle
traveling like a gift to him, all her challenges, her chest,
for instance, a private warning, its desires, plus
her weird, bad, bad love for fruit, it worries him.
What was he going to say? What was he thinking? He was
leaning in to name her parts, the salmon of her breasts,
the tips, flashing like a world, what did he mean,
what language would he say, *I saw, I see your shapes?*
Your fresh guile? Letters lining up to pair with each line of your mouth,
the *L*, for instance, its hard point, and the more applicable *M* and *O*,
against the vivid crash your cheekbone takes to air
and all that crazy, crazy, errant hair.

Satan must have been something,
his entrance dramatic, his lovely long form,
eye-catching, all his red, livid, hot
qualities. As the garden cooled, in he came.
The birds were quiet, the hills unmarked.
He came to the world like stealth, steady as lust,

and sunk deep, a solvent in the snake's skin,
tender as rain dreaming, a mist,
shapely and thin, his distillation,
his secret weather, and all over her
he came. Above her cool form,
the ether of him hovers,

pretty as a keepsake. Otherwise,
she would not have listened, or dreamed
to his will: the immaterial, the promises.
Otherwise, she would have been dreaming
the world as it was, and beyond her
the mountains would hang, vivid as church.

Instead, she is dreaming of tenuous bodies.
Instead, she is dreaming of the sea, crenelate, and of scallops,
hung in the waves, of suspension, of her weightless
form, of rare ideas, of trespass:
Take from the tree and eat. When she wakes,
the garden seems lambent,

strung with lights, like a party. She is wreathed
by mites, like powder, small luminaria,
impalpable trinkets, adornments, her evening's dress.
So taken, Eve rides Satan like a new car, and she rides
until Dad takes it away. He won't understand;
this will break His heart. But Satan's her first.

When he flatters, he flexes and wreathes,
his intricate flesh twisting with blood.
Sinuous, she coils like a replica.
She is ready to burst her skin at the crisp possibilities.
Juiced up, the garden shines like a fat corsage
for the prom, and she believes him.

And beautiful—did he tell that?
So that into the purified world as generous as salt
as breakable, as delicate, but not yet defined,

arises from perfection a temperate tree,
each leaf prepared to an upturning, to *transpire*
in the first definition: *give off vapor*

as a part of photosynthesis,
the beginnings of rain, the leaves about *to
breathe*, second definition, and third: *it came to light.*

Surrounded by this text, her pale
face seems leaf-like: a page bound in volumes
yet to be written. The red bare boldness of the fruit.

The yoke in companionship, the consent.
After all this, solace, urged by undulation
to the tips of trees. The fable of the white wet juice

as the definition of desire. *Come on.*
Consider her as an intake of breath, a cheekbone
wedge-shaped, cuneal, cuneate. The first letters.

Maybe he sees her transcribed; beside him, in the lucid wash
of vegetation, there are outlines, imprecisions,
a liturgy of meanings, vocables, her mouth—

Climbing the tree, or did they bend the limb downward?
the trespass, the transcendence: *pass beyond
a human limit.* Facile. Submissive, the fruit understands

the demands of its bare white flesh: *ripened ovaries
of a seed-baring plant. Issue. Offspring.*
Gives with the slightest gesture a turning

from the cicatrize; the skin, vagrant, humming,
is shiny. The air is thin, grows into fracture.
Threshold: when the mouth opens

and the whole thing just falls apart.
He might have looked at her, and thought—
for the first time—*you're no good for me,*

but like any man he loves the harvest. Furnished
at such a price, giddy with want,
the twitch of desire so sweet, and he's thirsty.

To lose one's chastity. Used especially of a woman.

Simple tracing of his hand at fruit skin.
Simple breaking of. Firm yielding to. Intransitives.

Suddenly the visible world.
Wound and the ripening. The persuasion of failure.

The fruit swollen from its bud. To great effect.
The turning loose in the chaste world. Blossom: *lovely and full of promise.*

The girl. Membrane. Tissue. The flesh.
Simple breaking of.

Overwhelmed maybe. Orchard set to ruin.
The first and last perfection.

The now unhoused distances.
They became impure.

The florescence of them as they bouquet, in leafy shape:
Cuneate their bodies; *see also* **decurrent, decussate**.

decurrent *adj. Botany.* How they must have loved. As she took another bite, he came up behind her as would a deer: their shy necks and then, the raising of them, and the strange, savage bliss. His arms around her, the way a small leaf, extending from its center, hugs the stem from which it grows—from the Latin *decurrere,* to run down the stem (he didn't know this word)—bit his lip as he held her, ran his hand, slow as rain, down her flank; she licked the last bit of fruit from her lip and started to turn, and then their scilla, their nerves, the veined maps of their interiors, began a bloom—spreading out, his pulse mapped his form *like a leaf's veining,* he thought, *from my center outward,* his fingers the edges on her edges. She was a frond, sweet flag of her, woody, grassy, mossy, she turned to show her silver, her maple, her dreamy underside. They didn't notice the rest: the pale glow loosening its tide, the first ashy rush, obscure, as they turned.

decussate *adj. Botany.* Natural as vegetation, he takes her in the garden, in the fruit's aftermath. She turns, and their bodies start to cross. He thinks of the stars, distant, and, in their parsing of the sky, slim and empty; it felt a surprise, the whelm that rose from his belly. He runs his hands down her like he was a leaf and she a stem, and they grow together, bound at his stem from her planting of it. They cross their bodies, the first of several repeated and languishing Xs, as do leaves arranged, decussate, one above, crossed by one below: torsos pulled away and staring, laughing, the new moist words they made; they didn't know what they were saying. From the Latin, *decussare*, from *decussis*, number ten, they were X-ing and X-ing, coming out of the ground, verdant as all they lived among. Not noticing, in their inhalations, in their sweet words or new muscles as they mirrored the arbors and vined and tilled, the innovative gray pasture of sky, the dim eclipse, as it approached them.

To assume an expression of disappointment:
His Face fell.

God's disappointments.
To enumerate:
1) sand
2) the birds hovered less than would be tranquil
3) rain could be problematic
4) once companions are introduced, the notion of aloneness
5) they had been designed with certain capacities (not to be used)
6) nothing about her body
7) her responses, though: that distant look at everything
8) her interests
9) He was disappointed
10) her vulva open like a new bloom
11) they were supposed to have been
12) incorruptible
13) yes, in spite of the design, like the peacock
14) who shows a glimmering fan, whose colors are unique,
15) who shines, displays its wealth. But it is meek.
16) He could enumerate these disappointments:
17) sand
18) birds
19) rain
20) the possibility of loneliness
21) their capacity
22) genitals, entirely
23) also want
24) all this
25) in the inscrutable grasses
26) their moving bodies, unfathomable
27) how to express: His Heart sank?
28) Reader, I am disappointed too. Before the exile
29) the chipmunk's belly was gray, gray brown, the gazelle
30) swift as the tiger. And rain, though problematic,
31) never fell with such weight, a retribution.
32) The little creature's new white belly,
33) that predators can see. He's never safe. Why so?
34) Purity, before the stain. To have had it,
35) and lost it. And loneliness
36) and doubt. The garden's final innovation.

To undergo a reduction in amount, degree, or value;
To diminish.

Then the exile: In a kind of decrescendo they walk from the full, airy paradise,
with lowered arms into the dense reckoning of the finite.

The breaking of them. Once expelled, the incomprehensible—
a copy of the garden in which they had walked, and versions, repeating,

of the human figure. Elision. Endless in imaginations, like a mirror reflecting
the angle of something in repeated forms, diminishing. Her isolate hunger returns,

with vowels, with panting syllables, with utterance inexhaustible.
A slurred, erasable sky lifts its skirt, a lesson in perspective,

the come-hither V wherein the world simply goes away.
The eye can't comprehend. This is new. Introduction of the abstract.

The declension of them. The rupture of all this. Thrown out of gear
from the tendrilous ever, into the great wide open.

Once expelled, they enter the astringent, abrasive,
heavy world. Disjunction:

the proposition of both landscapes, with the assertion
that only one is true.

To divide naturally. Used with *into*:
The specimens fell into three categories.

Fallen already, the infallible world
and its memory replaced by the fulcrum of words,
the accumulation of language. Into all this naming,

one thinks only of the remarkable, yet
in the wake of it, a kind of interior loveliness:
what would one say? Cuneiform gathered,

white as day. They had broken the surface of the water.
Followed by their repeated images. Words to words
collected in word books, in alphabetical order

to make one-dimensional, and linguate/literate, the three-
dimensional world. As if letters shaped with curves and cuts
can hum up the geometry as it measures in its sweet little mesh

of ink and pulp the arc of any flyer, the distance
that, on any given evening, is so touching
we can barely find the sound to catch it.

So they saved their letters, words, pretty as a box
in a series of books: *Abecedarium. Aevary.*
Catholican. Dictionary. Manipulus.

But the homesickness remains. When the planet looks away
across the fields, the dark lining of the day in repose.
I wish I could tell you. Like the dictionaries,

the earth is veil of the primary world.
There was the lush place, immaculate as lust.
Its disappearance burned into language.

Post-Eden, some titles of wordbooks:

Abecedarium. *noun.*
(In order.)

Into the alphabet of the eye
all the words

Alevary. *noun.*
(Beehive.)

making a honey
of the interior, sweet buzz of language,

Catholican. *noun.*
(Cureall.)

the holy compulsion on the soft white
dressed in its tongue of symbol,

Dictionary. *noun.*

its arrangement of letters,
the universe dressed
as a malleable creature

Manipulus. *noun.*
(A handful.)

scooped like water to the mouth,
the world in words

Medulla. *noun*
(A marrow or pith.)

treading inside the very bone,
it tries to mean, to wonder, at

Ortus. *noun.*
(Garden.)

all the variegations, text of flowers
on vines sincere: words for this flutter

Thesaurus. *noun.*
(Treasury, storehouse.)

>inside the fluttering heart,
>its text as a bracket of permutations,

Sylva. *noun.*
(A wood.)

>its terribly complicated self, the language
>beating, blurred, and quite belimbed, what grace,

Vulgar Book. *noun.*
(A common thing.)

>this grace, these graceful, fiery, brittle shields
>in the common world, inked memory
>of doves and clouds and something everafter.

transitive

—**fall back**. To give ground; recede; retreat.

In a series of poems I'm unable to write, a bride displays her interior,
asking a spray of flowers and ribbons to stand for her within,
for her foliate insides, her inner pinks, her whites and her coming losses:
a decoration, a display, an engraving—frilled, flush, wavering

—of her usefulness. Cream roses? Pale lilies? The powder in the flower,
their heady scents and furry stems surround her, chiming. Lily of the valley:
wedding bells ringing like a corona about the sweet bouquet.
And in its whiteness, or, *And in its vivid blush,*

the day begins. As I have thought in my imaginings. She steps
into delicate slippers, she runs to the camera, she declines toward the ground
and its manifestation of grass, toward all of what it means.
I'll give you this: I'm imagining. It was years before I would be born.

The photograph's flat lexicon's ungiving, its betrayal
of dimension. It could have been raining. They had to have loved,
given love, like fresh ideas, and the doorway behind
them swings out, in a ceremony, and all of the people

throw, I don't know . . . rice? Seed? The metaphor: Multiply.
Fruitfulness. In that arithmetic of culture. Surrounded by flowers,
carrying flowers. Enraged were the flowers, at their most heightened—
sexed and prepared to be beautiful, their symbolic openings.

My mother and father were married, and walked among the guests,
among the arbor, and found their bodies later slipped of clothing,
cool, rung to each other. The many, restless conjugations they would make,
against which, from a distance, perceptively curved,

the earth appears in miniature: lifelike, petaled, tossed, and floral, in midair.

—**fall for**. *Informal.*
1. To become infatuated with; fall suddenly in love with.
2. To be tricked or deceived by; be taken in by.

At first not frail because she was younger. At first comprised
of flesh and thought, brim as a basket of nectarines
and the things of girldom, pearled, strong,

against the deciduous seasons, their losings of leaves,
their going away, a chastening, their slow descent,
baptizing the ground on which the solid flesh

walks out, conflicted: satisfied, yearning.
Against the long stem of flawlessness, they married,
and little girls threw petals, whites and reds

fluttering beneath the eye, sailing, cadence
like the inside of a woman, where everything is secret,
where everything returns, her envelope, her awning, the fertile,

furtive clock of her, inner pinks cloistered,
and full of prayer, oh how one wants to be.
Against the illusion of the grassy world,

how it curves when you drive on it, promising,
untying the unseeable, the unbelievable, as it emerges: who knew?
The earth slopes down. Within the *yes* of her she is a lake,

ruddle of animal, holographic, the *yes* of her dwindling
under her canopy of skin. Inspired, the husband answers,
dressed only in his coat of wants, his teenage *yes,*

the customary planet of the body's hard attention, his love for her.
And parting her legs out of homesickness, the blind eclipse
of them, against the sky's departure. The many interpretations,

ciphering. *Not noticing, because not looking?* or
Not noticing, because not there yet: the inviolate,
indelible tattoo of cancer. It undulates,

displays itself in fracture, its geometric love of digging in
like a bad luck, a tracing of the Fall. The tragic earth
slopes down, and I express a wish in air:

the sufferings of loved ones iridesce,
turn out to be transcendent, traverse
like an embroidery, illuminate, emblossomed.

And reckless, invisible, I await the bloom,
with her among so many. But I see her:
pale, extraordinary, glorious, simplified: entire,

unadorned: lost of that birthmark:
relieved of that stain: articulate,
a pattern of air, and air.

—fall among. To come by chance into the company of.

At my birth, I broke the surface of the water;
then I heard the end of the garden, and
felt the sadness of the exile. I pushed, or was pushed,
and found the new world's skin, the gate, her private entrance,
my new world, then I became, was introduced
to all that would delight and annoy me,

leaned into the way out, felt light-headed,
the stirring of all that wet, the blood, the shame,
her being burst open. I fell among the family.
And backward from the paradise:
the sounds of lambs, a bleating in rhythm.
Trees, marginal, and emarginate leaves,

cloudless partial sky like a tide. All lost to me,
the urge of the reckless afternoons, insistent
in their distances, that *gone astray*
of what I dropped, so far behind me.
This poem should run backward:
My coming into being,

the heart beating in my conception,
the absence of my possibility, and then,
that fruit and its constant scent, its holy,
impossible gesture. That flesh trouble,
made of seed, of want, and underneath,
the hidden, small, fine printing.

—fall behind. To be in arrears.

Everything goes away at evening.
It is as if a dance has ended,
and we put on our velvet wraps, a little regretfully:
goodnight. The brute matter of the world curves back,

descends, wishes for something, blows the errant eyelash.
I know this partial shadow, this dusk, this demi-jour.
Nightfall: relentless, handsome, dressed for the date
in his jacket of grief: *dark, darker, darkest.*

The light is going away, the light, disappearing,
and with it, our emphasis on earthly concerns.
We retreat to sheer veneers and husks,
to vapor, charted by touch, sphere by little sphere,

the rosary of us. Outside, a rush of animal, palpable, audible,
footprints like motes in the garden, something we owe,
it bothers us. *Who's there?* We wake often and lacking,
into the transparent, occluded land.

And when I recline, give myself to gravity,
the dear subjectives burst invisible from me, in dream.
Like a sweet pet, I hover, leashed to flesh, the austere tether
of our lives. And hot with envy for the fragile,

grooved white shells of feather the angels use.
There was the garden, wherein we walked.
How did sorrow enter the world?
Toward morning, the first bird will speak,

trying the air with a tentative whir: *Is it so?*
The bird is tiny, sweet, held in the darkened palm
of land. The world was generous,
with fruit and seed, and gave him wings.

Now regret cools the tall grass,
the bending vines: somber, basilicate.
When animals lament, they sleep spread out,
or wander. In fitful searching for the solid kingdom,

we dream the rare, the spongy, toothy place,
the mainland, our immaterial.
We dream after the perished,
a somehow aerial view.

And the bird was born so—with wings. To lift up,
toward the Him of it. To rise out?
A kind of return, the red whir of them. Toward
what was promised. The lightened body, let go.

—**fall on** (or **upon**). To attack suddenly; ambush.

The breast designs a pliant, outward shape,
and raises a sweet mast. It wants to spill itself,
it wants to be a metaphor: the fullness of a heart—

the body's height, its pitch, its amplitude,
its tenor, compass, reach—and reaches out
to slope, regretfully, a liquid density, a lesson

in pure gravity, in sympathy
with all the other parts. It hangs
this calibration on the rib, that awkward,

stolen, rough-hewn bone (thrown out of man,
and landing. The female grew in secret,
tangled up as a wisteria

on that moist and chalky trellis,
and her body: winding, wondrous).
What blemish

from the tree of knowledge, in a spite,
rose up like vegetation
in this fresh, untroubled mass?

Once, in this realm of precious flesh,
in the beautiful, tender, tenacious breast,
my mother found a little knot,

a dense coagulate against
the floral canopy of skin,
like she was chosen

on a whim. Or: she was nectar, and the lump, a honeybee
who wanted to be full, and it fed against her veins
and split her cells, and all its tiny fur undid her.

She was as clear as world, and sinless,
though she lived among us like a broken promise.
Maybe it whispered in her ear and held her,

set its adventitious roots to grow because it loved her.
But I doubt it. The window by the bed
showed all the summer air spread out against the cool day

like a petri dish, and we were unaware then, still,
and then the leaves would green, turn in the night,
and cool themselves; the years would pass.

But we were falling then, the family. In a collective faint
our blood leaned out, to run away from us
whose little nests of heart could not contain

our kindred, allied, grieving forms. So, when she turned,
turned from the window to the sounds of us,
she might have thought of something, of a hope,

the little and the large, the way the world,
so full of imperfection, with its hard spots and its hurt,
is all the world we have. Or that the sky, so simple,

blue above us, is only sky, an envelope of air
and prismed light, beneath which, we,
the too too solid flesh,

will merely be. If only I could know
that when the light withdrew at dusk,
and she beheld the silhouette

it was a welcome. That the blues
and grays that spun it were a scented invitation,
and when we slipped her pallid form

into the afterward of ground, it was as cool as hands,
as fitting as a letter, and she knew that love
in all its form, its rich and angry self, though angrier,

had set out shoots and blossomed in the hurt, and grown
unwieldy as a rosebush, in the hot, intensive daughters,
in the husband's quiet stare. But bloomed, and filled the air.

—**fall away**. 1. To decline; languish; weaken.
2. To withdraw support; part company.

The day casts a loose, languid spell, a reckless,
forgetful lover, and I am undone again, hurt,
wet, fresh to its wantings. This secondary place,
its tertiary greenings, the expiration of the grasses
into my lungs, dressing me up inside.

I have left off from the wanting.
The days of squirrel skin and little graves,
of call and response, brimmed up
with amulets I cannot name:
hard, dark feather, headless crow.

The sacred losses, having fallen.
We cast off the bad memory
as a useless skin, and left it out by the fence,
crisp as straw. In evening, daylight decreasing
as afternoon begins to forget herself

and the vines, tenacious, desperate,
loosen their grasp, tendrils relaxing,
the vegetation shedding rain.
We loved the gardens,
so pregnant, emerging. But then they grew fallow

and sloped with their weight, like the necks
of the deer at the end of the season, skinny
and haunted. So breathtaking, so ready
for their end. Like any gorgeous thing,
they'll fall away.

—**fall under**. To succumb to;
come under an influence or power.

Outside in floral, vegetating thought,
the empty spaces fill with world.
The fitful budding of the columbine,
and intricate, demure, wild growth that wanders
where it wants. Daylilies sugar up in blur.

These scarlets and these yellows tongue and hover
in my version of the world. I try to notice lilies,
try to paraphrase their blooming.
(*The blossoms lift like children;*
they look up.) I tell them

how the words I use are useless,
and dragonflies form laterals in air:
their spider's web of body, touching down;
and still they float around in parity: their gravity,
the weight of sky. I love their wings

like heaven, glassy patterns in the air,
above the air. Against the upward thrust of earth,
I lay my fragile figure down, eye-level
to the latitude of leaf. Imagine plants,
who promise to remain as if a gift, unwrapped,

but at the season's end they take it back,
and wither, and hardly say goodbye.
Then we are waiting only for the vaster shapes to come,
the bright, descending creatures
and their emblems: their lambent,

lacy wings. My mother was blade-thin,
as thin as blade, and scattered to the wind
as seed, and left us all she had:
the final shell of her, the lace of her,
veined like a wing.

I cannot find her anywhere,
against the breeze, unnoticed, wild,
or the netting of the trees at nightfall.
*(The blossoms lift out of the ground,
and we look up.)* The garden is the dream of loss,

a drift of cell and stem, and gone, a petaled dress
of scent and pollen. Is she among
the far-off limbs and secret trees,
and missing fields towards which I turn,
out of my homesickness as blue as bruise?

Or out of love: that reckless, gentle thing
that hangs its head, that shifts the family leeward.
It torques and fissions, that which spun me,
slim hot thread of cell division.
(The sadness of the petals, looking.)

—fall foul. To become entangled.

This morning; four pale globes of fruit.
Tomato plants we grew from seed

(I watched the vague blind petiole, the stalk,
a little fist, curl from its husk.)

Squirrels quarrel in the walnut tree, their tack of claws
on bark. They argue out a limb

and make it writhe, and leaves
float down to me; they're giving up.

The lilies were all bud: smooth, green, and closed,
like healing skin. But as the days go on,

the calyx shifts, and opens like a mouth:
a wounded pair of lips that, tearing back,

reveals hot sugars in the reds, their orange shapes,
and pierce the eye. Their haughty anthers hurt:

thin filaments of lust. And vines extend their legs
like naughty girls. When they are ripe and full,

fruits fall away, but keep the cicatrize, the wound.
The world is coming into vibrant, painful bloom.

Trying to say (about the sadness, the failures):
A fat bird instructs with his stiletto singing
to the tree's fallings, its several losses,

limbs tossed from the hard, constant summers,
the winds of distinct attention, also the rains,
slapping at us, the doom of them at the door.

While the small un-treed limb,
the baby fruit, separates, hits the ground;
the yard littered with leavings, out of necessity:

in the grains of the world's vision only so much room,
only enough light, the randomness. For what
does the world offer, do we deserve?

To find its several colored losses.
I want to know the whys of it, the unfairnesses.
Its semivague eyes, its knowing of us, etc.

That she died we have no argument.
That it is tragic, we have no argument.
That it was simple, a goodbye, we understand most

at evening, the reminder of the leave-taking,
of the day (Oh please don't go)
shadows lengthening (the true cliché) until the house

is gloom. It takes forever to adjust. To what is offered.
The world offers its losses: intricate, impersonal,
the daily exiles, exhausting.

Out of the house I want her back.
Out of the yard I want her back.
Out of the traffic I wish her back.

Out of the birdsong purled and knit to the air
I wish for her return. Pass through into the garden.
Pass the others through, losing our stain.

I want her to beckon, rise out from her illness,
tear through the curtain of the injured body. I want
all the families shattered by the Eve

to reknit. The myth of it.
I want all the broken passages mended.
These are errant, useless, impossible words.

Into the house, the world's green
is a screen of the wounded, the clasped hands of the leaves,
birds, praying at morning, the trill so little

against the unknown, but it rises,
giddy, thin, atomic, and hopeless:
life accumulates losses while elsewhere, happiness: that's all.

—**fall back on** (or **upon**).
1. To retreat to. 2. To resort to.

Another season casting like bouquets its sterling losses,
whose leaves curl at the crenate edge, who wither
on the stem. And should we take them down,
or let them die there, as they wish?

I am letting the yard stand for the world, as dreary
as that seems. The grasses and the tree articulate,
engraved as fine as early printing.
Initials cut of tin and inked in leaf, the yard

a manuscript of tropes, its human figures,
animals and urns entwining, its two-color of birds,
who sing, in register, their glossy, pointed wings.
The cross strokes of the tallest trees, and counterspace

of nest; the brilliant, cursive world lets go.
I am letting the seasons stand
in a reckless cliché, for us: hard grammars
of our childhood, handwritten, toward

the longhand, adult autumn, when she
defined herself into the sky,
and all was lost. Then fall came, early
and unwelcome, its dossier of weathers

and its flirty grays and browns.
Once, all but sheathed under the rains,
I wandered out, against the naked cells of plants
and surface tension. I pierced through her, perfoliate,

spread up to find the family. They are cast off.
The seasons are like losses: the skeletons of insects,
and hot, overdone roses. And words, who miss the body's
bruised human embrace.

Clean sheets, fresh medicine, and glittering brown
bottles, full with liquid drugs. Cutting us adrift,
where privacies occur, the bleak waves' measure,
and doctors, whose ornate masculine cartographies
would navigate my mother's darkening seas.
The nurses in the halls were starchy skiffs, like paper boats.

It unpolished us, took down the house eave by eave,
splintering the doorways, through which
the world began. The current draws us toward collision:
to know the teenaged drift of losing her, our long, white afternoons,
dismantling, and she: the far-flung, worthy shore.

Last night, drowsy at the growing vegetation:
The heathy vines that overwhelm the porch.
Black walnut, its exquisite earthliness, and I look up.
These shapes our longings take. Now daylight
troubles me, it asks me to remember

the way it was before: her several years of health.
Outside, the seashell-tinted birds, like flares, erupting
at sweet interval, attempt interpretations,
misinterpret. The second world is such a beauty
with its many gifts and losses. It's something. It goes on.

—fall to. 1. To begin (a physical activity) energetically.
2. To shut or move into place by itself.

Is it exhaustion that lets the body wander,
and travel at infinite degree
toward wanting? Leashed to the myth
with what's remaindered:

feral planets of desire that punctuate,
like commas, the long phrases of our wanting.
Dreaming hurts at the ripped seams of it,
and I dream. Across the yard

the beautiful endures
in brutal, climacteric trees.
They loosen at the limbs, a loss of memory,
and as the things descend

they say a prayer about their fall.
And some leaves twitch like feeling at the light,
and close themselves against all touch,
this motor impulse I admire.

While I might open out, like tongue,
I'll snap to my within
as swift as touch, and red as underskin,
a darkened mouth, and wish the fill of it.

At night, the husband wanders,
carries in his arms like flowers his vast love,
and I begin a bloom for him—
with all my silly flesh, the rest of it,

in spite of, or because our human love
—the complicated body of dimension—
it's just too rich, we all but haul it up
in these electrical disturbances and shapes:

the braiding of our lungs, their candied net,
striated muscle, and little hearts
as soft as birds—these private,
bright assays against a calendar of myth and stain,

against the immaterial they also love. The body
is devout, and when we are entwined of limb,
we look like praying hands, we shape our faith,
we marvel in the imitated world.

noun

—n.

That which has fallen.

from grace: nothing that is unredeemable:
in the world there is the real and then the brilliant crush of thought:
being flesh and bone we recognize our kindred,

by their winks and ticks: the dream of the inhabitance,
the high holy days of the mind: what we could have been:
we are inoculate with wanting: spread out to our ends

like a sea tide, our pulse and blood the traveler,
little Magellan to our inner pinks, our marrow:
all the same, the dreams of kindness: dreams of wings and rising up:

in spite of the heft of us: our spiritus aeris lingua franca:
our inner boat on our systolic wave: last night I read
we can have wings attached for the purpose of beauty:

the divine final flight back to the ether of us:
I would spread out from the shoulder blades and lift:
and the grief would be a companion,

resting on the upper frame of the arc of the wing, spread out:
it can sustain the weight of me: against
the horizontal weight that keeps us earthbound:

homesickness: to fly, to touch the hands of those:
whose hands we miss so dearly: in their last station:
the move into the state of grief, with all its boxes ever packed:

glancing down to see the first world: having known
the absolute, now, the absolute breadth
of the metaphorical world: that bears it: up: it lifts

to explicate the angelic: with words

Usually capital **F.** *Theology.* Adam's sin of disobeying God
by eating the forbidden fruit in the Garden of Eden, and the
consequent loss of innocence and grace of all his descendents.

First the dark cloud. Then the first guilt, and in the mouth,
a reckless dream of sweetness. Oh but we loved it,
and kept the disobedience as pure as was the paradise

of afternoon, its colors private and its weather of one.
After the transom crossed, the loss of all we could say to one another,
and to the father, who now resides in the hereafter,

and he wishes to speak; to say, *I miss you;* but his face
is turned like a mountain, tuned to a differing sense of the world,
and what we have are the leavings of wishing.

If such a thing happened. If such a thing exists. The tongue is an eye:
language is an eye: it speaks a dream of loss: it hastens to a thing not said:
it knows the way home but will not speak it: it sees the fever

and the sullen life: it tastes the idea of memory: it recites us from memory:
it holds us: it babies us: it pretends to know the secrets:
it pretends to keep the world: it refreshes with its weakness:

it loves its futile soundings: it plays with meaning as if a child:
it tells a joke to entertain us, to say I love you, I miss you,
while all the landscapes apprehend without the miserable, impossible tongue:

it dissembles: it believes: it hisses: it soothes with false kisses
on the inside of the ears, and lips still dressed with latent sugars:
it dresses our evenings with want: it hovers: it leaves

when the soul appears: it sounds as though it will be the one to rise, all dream, all
gesture: to that something, that one possession we left behind:
to apprehend with our mouths the world:

when we left the first home we inherited this language:
when I felt the first juice of red trouble cross my tongue I thought,
How can I say this? How would I know this?

A sudden drop from a relatively erect
position to a less erect position:
He fell to his knees.

n. 1. A reverent petition made to a deity or other object of worship.
2. The act of making such a petition. 3. Any act of communion with
God, such as confession, praise, or thanksgiving. 4. a specially worded
form used in addressing God. 5. *Often plural.* Any religious service
in which praying predominates. 6. Any fervent request. 7. The thing
so requested: *His safe arrival was their prayer.* 8. *Law.* a. The request
of a complainant, as stated in a bill in equity, that the court grant the
aid of relief solicited. b. The section of the bill that contains this re-
quest. [Middle English *preyere*, from Old French *preire*, from Medi-
eval Latin *precāria*, written petition, prayer, from Latin, feminine of
precārius, obtained by entreaty, from *precāri*, to entreat, PRAY.]

An ornamental cascade of lace or trimming
attached to the dress, usually at the collar.

In a wedding, the veil overwhelms: a haze, a halo,
the gesture angelic, misty, it transforms:
its grille of white: this lends the yard a purity:

in the garden, the lilies were endless: yoked, gasping, exhaling sugars
against the afternoon: the day just a breath now, and someone's voice:
the tulips looked surprised, the curve of their lips:

the dress caked the bride in frost, all icing, all stiff, hard fabric,
and underneath, the invisible aspects of blood, like a calling:
the bride wanted to seem: white as a dove; white as a flower;

white like wish; like a wistful moon; she said *I will be the day*:
I will find in my bearing the words to say:
I have made on this earth a promise to love:

and the outside world pretended to know her,
to shape itself from her mind, where the clouds
were like imagined clouds: the harvest in the trees hung like waiting,

and sorrow held its breath at the core:
the deeply repentant apple, blameful, full of seed:
crisp because it knows from whence it came:

crisp with the ache for one last look:
the fruit of the garden sends it regrets:
how full of promise seems this world, against its contract of gravity:

too-fragile axis of apple stem:
transitive arc of the conjugal bouquet:
erosion of birdvoice across transoms of air:

translation of the earth:
sustained:
suspended:

The amount of what has fallen.

And this one for me, across that other, imagined transom:
the things the lost world says, it says: welcome home.
Mother as thin as the earth's frail blessing,

out of the envelope of promise,
that day when you left, regretfully, the family,
and hovered, all the sheets were white, all our blood

seemed white in what was lost:
the parting, the divine just taken out of me
from your pale form and *she flew into the trees,*

above the trees, and gestures:
I only see the shapes: *I am not,*
she says, *I am not* but I can only see the shapes

against the curve of this madness, the comprehensible earth,
and its partner, beauty, the world's diversion:
tree's bright-limbed intensity against the division of the sky:

the bright shapes of her hair, sharp cheekbone,
the eye of lake, of gentle stone. The first innocence broken,
we could go nowhere else, nor return home.

The breaking of all skin and bone and muscle,
just to reach that castle of a heart: and when she left,
I felt the boat glide off without me:

above me, still, her strands of hair
grow into leaves, to limbs,
and honeyed birds can rest into the sky: what does she say?

But I discern her moves *Things*
are not as they appear. The beautiful
endures. I love. I am not

I am not trapped here

The end of a cable, rope, or chain that is pulled
by the power source in hoisting.

The repetition, with shaped variation,
of sunlight refreshing the eastern trunk of the pines
in a metaphor for God. Moss's metaphor for God
to blanket the fallen gray of the forest trees.
The deer turns her head as a metaphor for God
in the wild edge of the disordered wood.

White-throated sparrow thrice locates her metaphor for God
in the distillation of thin, wondering breath,
high pitch emerged from a mix of her thinking, the singing,
in her small wet heart, and beating its arc in uncertain richness
to touch, in increasing, diminutive lessenings—
as snowfall, as fabric furled out, as a hand through the breeze

feels the presence of other—the air only seeming acceptance,
to let birdsong travel: meanwhile, extending their bodies
they feather the present tense, the moment, the turbine,
foreseeable hushed in the eye, to try the air
as conduit for finding, with treble song: *once, twice, verify.*
Against such a desire, the land extends whatever it has

to the upward, the visual above, which gilds the wondering,
where air erodes to some attenuated rapture, a gap where meaning
gathers up its flaws. Against this persistence, bird song
falling, repeated patterning, over other holy gestures,
other estimations: a water strider proves
the surface tension of the metaphor for God

is equal to his reverent body in the blue dark underneath.
Seraphic ferns undo themselves in Prime
by looking upward, compose their leaves in evening's
Compline metaphor for God. Though an open window
cool air compels itself to
warmer air's metaphor for God.

Asking only this.

The act or an instance of falling;
a dropping down; free descent.

Out of all of it, the unreckless and severe together,
are these graces: the nonsense of love,
and of the pretty flowers to entrance us:

the metaphors emerge wet and new
from their quite unsheathed skins: the details,
in their accumulation, the quilt of it, each stark stitch

lulled to stitch, simply the tension that will hold,
cloth on soft cloth, the whole damn thing together.
And when they buried the body,

placed it low under the surface of the walking world,
we could be startled by the glamour of the headstone,
its gray so unlike her, so cold and with a gloss

in places where they polished it. We could be startled again
by the gape in the grass, its punctuation in the day,
by the sound—the sound! like nothing else—

of that first clump of dirt, falling back to itself,
reuniting. Around us, the faces, and bodies,
full of something, tender half-circlet of blood, braceleting,

against which we imagine the absence of it all,
against which—because unknowing—we imagine
the atmosphere, pink, soft, rarified:

The birth of an animal, especially, the birth of a lamb.

How the surface shivers so as to guide those breaking through.
And see the fracture there—translucent
in the body's hot parenthesis, where love's wet seeds
transfigure, strip, are bare, begin a flaw.

At birth, interior—exposed—enters new land,
is rinsed of prelude. What choice is there?
An innocence remains, a love of vanished gardens with all the boundaries knit,
and the persistent echo, fresh, of something,

once removed, once released,
if perfect, if incomplete—

—

—a gate swings slowly shut behind.

A seed breaks from its coat out of a thirst,
and sets out roots, and wanders for survival.
There in the tree's rich span, the apple flower, hovering, decides.
See how she breaks to petal in a nuptial white,

the bloom who is transfixed to fixity.
Persistent, she deceives;
obsessed with her endurance, the petals make-believe to want
the spinefold legs of bee, they make-believe it's all for him;

they look the other way and write a lust on air,
they flirt a musk in labial skirts,
pink-open whites of desperate mouth the bee finds
irresistible. The petals know too much about the bee.

I love the bee, his hurt desire, his weak whim to the nectaries,
I love his wants on her, the dizzy thrusts low to her hollows,
where anthers yield the pollen as encumbrance.
A minuscule weight against impediment of air.

And see the insect there, rare hover
in the naked inflorescence.
It's worth it in the cluster to let his body go into a loss
for such as this: quick-scented sex, drunk folly of allure.

He'll have to try another, won't he, to find
the absolute in what is rich, for him. It's unavoidable; it's hunger;
it's pattern; it's design. He brushes the stigmata
with pollen-sodden legs. His industry, his labors:

strange perfume of the work.
Fruit swells its flesh within the arguments of botany,
breaks the integument because of lust,
in spite of vivid ruin: the lessening of bloom

for everything. The way to such perfection is a series
of quiet, violent acts. Now petals, roseate, fade to white,
and in irregular display, descend, and leave behind
the first, the red, the pretty fruit.

Intermission

: across the territory of the subjective, with words,
I invest a fermata, gel the world into a firmness:
And see the reckless eye of bee, astigmatic

in the sweetness, pendent in the inbetweens,
devout to the flower's cloistered cell.
Through a hitch in time, fermata:

hitch in the fabric there: threads,
isolate, of petals chilled and highly visible,
fragile tear cross-magnified to the afternoon's withholdings.

He had to come to rush the nectary,
presuming metatarsus into recesses,
arguing his frenzy for corolla, calyx,

the team designed to hold him there for long enough
and then release the thing to fly midrange and strike again.
I want to intercept this one cross-pollination:

an interlude of words, to disagree the bridge
between the bony hot trochanter, the fringe of him,
and vast (now magnified here, lush

and luscious in the grammar of stillness, waiting)
yellow, grainy, hurting field. I fix in time a stop-time:
This atmospheric still-shot of the honey bee

inert above the matching frame,
distracted play of bloom.
Yet untouched,

yet undisheveled.
Wherein persists the punctuated world,
the apple forever interrupted. (Imagine.) Then what

would Adam want for? Or where would fall
Eve's glance? A tree of gentle blossoms shades the couple,
blurred as meaning, as a rain, against

the bodies of the grass blades, against forgetting.
The couple spends the day inhaling air
in which a single sparrow, blessèd, hovers.

(Wait for it.) (Something.) I would distract the bee
to keep the world ajar. Against which
the *what-if?* of our disorder. Against the meanwhile, running

and—inevitable—the physics of alighting.

The apple blossom hung at the end of something,
a calendar hung in a beauty, a beauty
dressed in a silence, the word never having been uttered,

in kindness, in solitude, before churches,
before the answering architecture of our searches
pointing, nearly always, splendidly upward,

extending, against a sky of deep, inhaled indifference.
And somehow it was imagined they would be good.
So had alighted insect. So had confided insect

to the blossom, whispering proboscis
in blossom hollow. So the apple enjoyed a mineral longing
as the petals washed about.

If the bee (thinks the apple) *didn't alight,*
if the bee (thinks the apple) *never wanted.*
What kind of world is that to flourish in?

If I let x = *want, if I let* y = *beginning;*
then x *(the amount the blossom knew to love me)*
and y *(the potential of innocence);*

therefore x *(possibility) over* y *(surrender).*
And its tangents:
the two of them, admiring my fair shape,

the pleasure of the currents of wind,
amid a disobedience, kissing me
on my kissing mouth.

When Eve finally turned to regard me,
when she reached for me, I felt fragile, delicate,
drained, perceiving. I watched the daylight
steer itself into extravagant shapes:
long, slow veronica of elements flaring,
the distance burgeoning, almost a blur; and I broke free.

A downward movement or slope.

The freedom in the unmoored world is gesture
we must make toward a belonging. As every leaf
prepares for its abscision on a branch of heathered leaves.

Though air supports the slow descent, the spiral of their questionings,
the evidence is all abstract: my testing, loving, curious kingdom,
my lucky days, my strange existence, pale and thin in search of God.

Leaves—the palmate hand of something—vascular,
leafmeal vein of the divine, breathing: preoccupied.
Outside, the porch is bursting with bright lilacs, so cumbersome with beauty,

above which mere gray birds try song, like me:
to hear the echo bouncing off of something hidden: the trees,
above the trees, throughout the trees, against the trees, beyond them.

I'm wrong sometimes, in the magnolias, grassblades,
hollows, fallen things, all tender on my hurt mouth's wish.
In each day's mend, and each day's tear, forbearance:

and I would give the whole of it, sometimes, out of my love—
inclement world so chastened by the mercies,
as is the cactus by its flower, cereus blooms who open up for me

just in the far too dark, and in whose search I am uncertain longing.
My night bloom opens too, as fracture for a mouth,
as fragrance: I pray the pattern holds me.

The leaves are naked, they diminish, and in their travels,
persists a bliss at all the wide impermanence.
Deciduous, attached, the pigment loves its givens:

hot moisture and its sugars, its coming yellows, scarlets,
crimsons, bloods, in leaves respirant, fertile,
spiny, and elliptic: fall then.

It is abscision. Fall. Witnessing, bowing, traveling,
lessening, migrants, firm, evergreen,
and done with it, leaving,

freed, passing, desiring, torquing, swifting,
perhaps knowing, perhaps never knowing,
my visible, my invisible, my shade, my search, my reasons;

the scent of coming seasons, and time, his imperceptible hot kiss.
Above, there, robins ride on tender branches, consider with their heads
the brittle birch. They sing, asking or telling . . . making, anyway,

spare beauty, imperfect, in imperfect wonder.
Are they abashed, to show their rust hearts so?
They sing: the leaves descend.

Often capital F. Autumn.

Ripe and overripe, the fleshy fruit and their late year scents,
their severing of cicatrices, at the wound of stem.
The yard has the mind of ending, like the first long walk away,

the decrescendo of the birds, the last thought of the tulips,
waxed and patterned, heads bowing. As the garden goes away,
it bends, it falls, dilutes the sun, its brilliant eye,

against the tree limbs, hung above us, the memory of the first place,
blooming. Against a latent dream of loss, there was the beautiful,
the body and the God, the doves, the slow incumbency of world.

That we had given up for want, for a crisp note in a dark sky,
to love by now this clear, legible copy. It's what we have.
The day droops down, the sky will bend its neck at night,

its darkness is a scent to us and when the trees relent,
their limbs fall out: the languor of their curves is sweet,
and birds will rush to feed where they can rest,

between their parings and their song:
they swift on waves of air, on fallen waves, and bodies
mesh their lessenings like leaves, and intergrate a sense

of something downward, and we know it, in the way
we bury mothers, fathers, in the wound of land: a planting
of the husk: above, against blue scrim of sky, we hope

into a bloom, brisk of petal, pink as an apple flower, frilled
as the memory of loss, its scent so apple-sweet, so sweet of apple
flesh and all the world has missed: and love, not just the word:

the blossom breaks apart: it rains a blessing,
like seed at a wedding: it is the fruit's beginning, and I
am still on earth, the deep wet earth: I live here.

I walked alone beyond the yard: the afternoon
was brilliant, was syntactic underneath the leaves;
it slayed me. I wish I could tell you.

Notes

Definitions of the words "fall" and "prayer" are taken primarily from *The American Heritage Dictionary of the English Language* (Houghton Mifflin, 1979).

The epigraph by Rainer Maria Rilke is from the first elegy in Edward Snow's translation of *The Duino Elegies* (Northpoint; Farrar, Straus & Giroux, 2000).

The history of the names of wordbooks in "To divide naturally. Used with *into: The specimens fell into three categories*" and "Appendix[c]" is found in Jonathan Green's *Chasing the Sun: Dictionary Makers and the Dictionaries They Made* (Henry Holt, 1996).

The phrase "the tongue is an eye" in "Usually capital **F**. *Theology.* Adam's sin of disobeying God by eating the forbidden fruit in the Garden of Eden, and the consequent loss of innocence and grace of all his descendants" is from Wallace Stevens's "Adagia."

About the Author

Amy Newman is an Associate Professor of English at Northern Illinois University. She is the author of two books of poetry: *Order, or Disorder* (Cleveland State, 1995), which received the Cleveland State University Poetry Center Prize, and *Camera Lyrica* (Alice James Books, 1999), which received the Beatrice Hawley Award.

Library of Congress Cataloging-in-Publication Data

Newman, Amy (Amy Lynn)

Fall / Amy Newman.

   p. cm.

ISBN 0-8195-6708-6 (cloth : alk. paper)

I. Title.

PS3564.E9148F34 2004

811'.54—dc22   2004052612